# Common Sense

## Michael De Medeiros

Published by Weigl Publishers Inc.
350 5th Avenue, Suite 3304, PMB 6G
New York, NY 10118-0069
Website: www.weigl.com

Library of Congress Cataloging-in-Publication Data

De Medeiros, Michael.
 Common sense / Michael De Medeiros.
    p. cm. --  (World of wonder)
Includes index.
 ISBN 978-1-60596-062-3 (hard cover : alk. paper) -- ISBN 978-1-60596-063-0 (soft cover : alk. paper)
 1.  Common sense--Juvenile literature.  I. Title.
 B105.C457D43 2010
 152--dc22
                                    2009001963


Printed in China
1 2 3 4 5 6 7 8 9 0  13 12 11 10 09

Editor: Heather C. Hudak
Design and Layout: Terry Paulhus

All of the Internet URLs given in the book were valid at the time of publication. However, due to the dynamic nature of the Internet, some addresses may have changed, or sites may have ceased to exist since publication. While the author and publisher regret any inconvenience this may cause readers, no responsibility for any such changes can be accepted by either the author or the publisher.

Every reasonable effort has been made to trace ownership and to obtain permission to reprint copyright material. The publishers would be pleased to have any errors or omissions brought to their attention so that they may be corrected in subsequent printings.

Weigl acknowledges Getty Images as it primary image supplier for this title.

# CONTENTS

4    What is Common Sense?

7    Using Your Common Sense

8    Back in Time

10   Brain Power

13   Thinking Parts

14   Putting It to Action

16   Making Choices

18   Animal Habits

20   Acting on Instinct

22   Test Your Common Sense

23   Find Out More

24   Glossary/Index

# What is Common Sense?

How do you make choices? Common sense is when you make good choices based on **experience** and what you know to be true. Everyone has some common sense.

**Senses** help us experience the world around us. There are five basic senses. These are sight, taste, smell, touch, and hearing.

# Using Your Common Sense

When it is raining, do you put on a raincoat? Do you look both ways when crossing a street? Often, you do these things without thinking. When this happens, you are tapping into your common sense.

You know from experience that rain will make you wet. You put on a coat to keep dry. You also know you might get hurt if you walk into traffic. This is why you look both ways before crossing a street.

# Back in Time

Have people always known about common sense? The first person to talk about common sense was a Greek **philosopher** called Aristotle. He was born nearly 2,400 years ago, in 384 BC.

Aristotle said that the five senses join to form common sense. He said that people have different types of common sense. This is because it is based on what they are taught. It is also based on their own experiences.

9

# Brain Power

How does your brain turn thoughts into actions? Your ears, eyes, skin, nose, and mouth send thoughts to the **cerebrum**. When you think about kicking a ball, the cerebrum controls the muscles you need to do this.

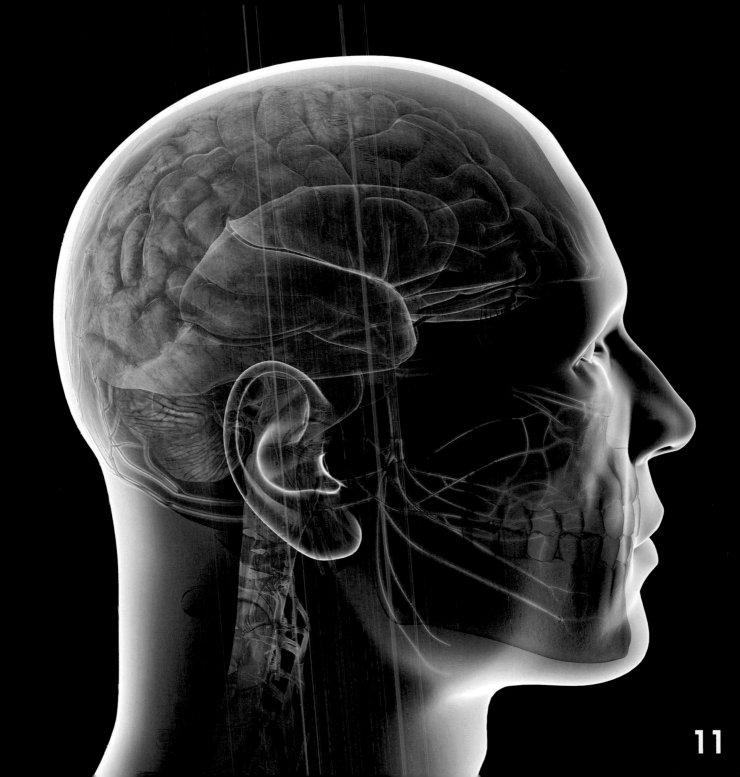

# Thinking Parts

What part of your brain does the thinking?
Most thoughts take place in the cerebrum.
It is the biggest part of the brain.

A signal is sent from the cerebrum to
the other parts of your brain and body.
Then, those other body parts
take action.

The cerebrum helps you
solve problems and
answer questions.

# Putting It to Action

How many thoughts did you have today? People have 50,000 to 60,000 thoughts each day. Common sense is a part of almost every thought we have.

Common sense tells us how to act. You can tell a burner on a stove is hot just by looking at it. Common sense tells you that, if you touch it, you could get hurt.

# Making Choices

When was the last time you made a choice? Did you have the tools you needed to make a good choice?

Think about the first time you ate an ice cream cone on a hot day. You may have become sticky. This is because you did not know to lick the drippings. The next time, you knew to lick around the edges.

Once you have an experience, you can use what you now know to make a good choice.

# Animal Habits

How do animals make choices? Birds and great apes may be able to think about the past and the future. They may use this knowledge the same way humans use common sense. **Research** is being done to learn more.

It is likely that animals use their other senses to help them make choices. Scientists are trying to learn more about animals and how they use their senses.

# Acting on Instinct

What does it mean to act on instinct? Instinct is a **natural** response. It is not based on what you have learned. Common sense can be confused with instinct.

Instinct is something you are born with. Some instincts are shared by all people. This may include knowing when to eat or sleep.

Instinct can be wrong. You may think you are tired or hungry, but your body may not need sleep or food. Common sense is based on what you have learned. It has less chance of being wrong.

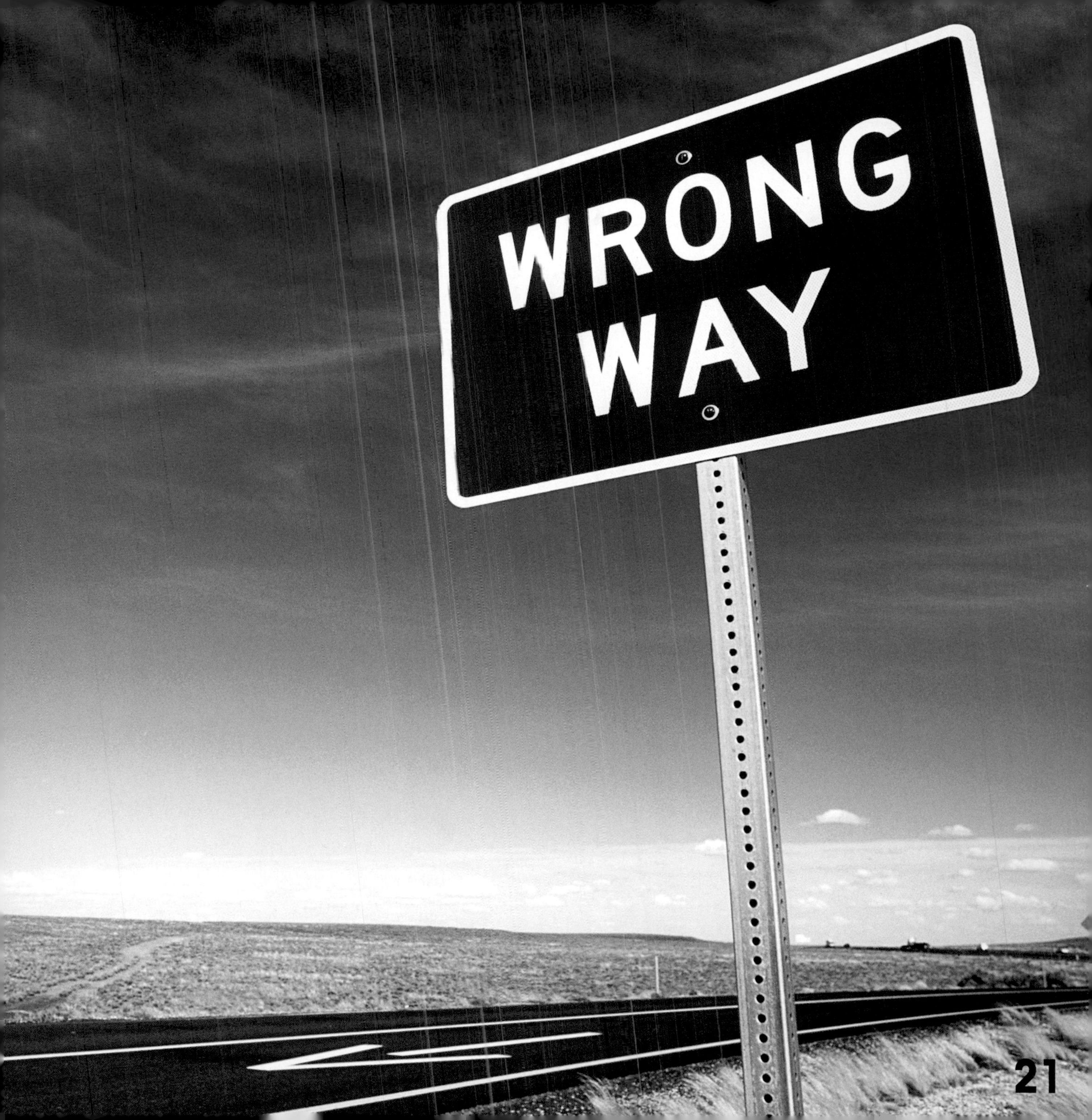
WRONG
WAY

# Test Your Common Sense

**Supplies**
notebook, pencil

1. Make three columns in the notebook. Label one "Common Sense," another "Instinct," and the last "Other."

2. Think about everything you did today. Decide which acts used common sense, instinct, or something else. Write that action in the proper column.

3. For each action, write down how you made your choice to act a certain way.

# Find Out More

To learn more about common sense, visit these websites.

**Kids Philosophy Slam**
www.philosophyslam.org/
1_27.html

**Neuroscience for Kids**
http://faculty.washington.edu/
chudler/chsense.html

**Your Brain & Nervous System**
http://kidshealth.org/
kid/htbw/brain.html

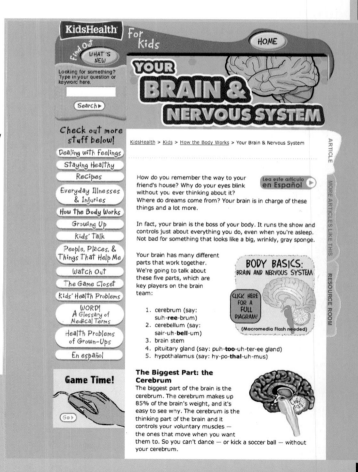

# Glossary

**cerebrum:** the biggest part of the brain

**experience:** things that a person lives through or does

**natural:** a certain skill that people and animals are born with

**philosopher:** someone who studies a subject and talks about what it means

**research:** to study something in detail

**senses:** the ways the body gets information about what is happening in its surroundings

# Index

actions  10, 14, 20, 22
animals  18
Aristotle  8

cerebrum  10, 13

experience  4, 7, 8, 16

instinct  20, 22

learn  18, 20

thoughts  10, 13, 14